MINDSET MAGICK

*Uncover & Uproot Subconscious &
Unconscious Blocks to
Health, Happiness & Success*

Frances Douglas

First published by Busybird Publishing 2018
Copyright © 2018 Frances Douglas
ISBN 978-1-925692-53-2

Frances Douglas has asserted her right under the Copyright, Designs and Patents Act 1988 to be identified as the author of this work. The information in this book is based on the author's experiences and opinions. The publisher specifically disclaims responsibility for any adverse consequences, which may result from use of the information contained herein. Permission to use information has been sought by the author. Any breaches will be rectified in further editions of the book.

All rights reserved. No part of this publication may be reproduced, stored in or introduced into a retrieval system, or transmitted in any form, or by any means (electronic, mechanical, photocopying, recording or otherwise) without the prior written permission of the author. Any person who does any unauthorised act in relation to this publication may be liable to criminal prosecution and civil claims for damages. Enquiries should be made through the publisher.

Cover image: Franie D
Cover design: Busybird Publishing
Layout and typesetting: Busybird Publishing

Busybird Publishing
2/118 Para Road
Montmorency, Victoria
Australia 3094
www.busybird.com.au

Disclaimer
The methods described within this book are the author's personal thoughts. They are not intended to be a definitive set of instructions and you may find there are other methods and materials to accomplish the same end result.

This book is not intended to be a substitute for the medical advice of a licensed physician. The reader should consult with their doctor in any matters, relating to his/her health.

Firstly, I dedicate this book to my beautiful mum, Valera, who passed away suddenly on 21 March 2017.

This one is for you, Mum! I know how much you were looking forward to my first book coming to fruition and how proud you were of me!

Secondly, I dedicate this book to all those who truly wish to elevate themselves & their lives to their greatest, healthiest, happiest and most successful potential and reality.

Acknowledgements

With infinite gratitude I acknowledge and thank my inner sacred circle of family and friends who have always believed in me and seen the blinding light of my divinity – even when I could not – for without them, this book would not be and my words and photographs would never have been made public. There are some people I'd like to particularly thank!

Firstly, I want to thank my youngest child and son – Connor Douglas – for his unwavering unconditional love, support, comfort, care, encouragement and belief in me, through my darkest years!

I thank my daughter and son – Briana Kent and Kane Douglas – for their love and for inspiring me to be my true and authentic self!

I thank my wonderful friend and kindred spirit – Melissa Jones – for her ability to give selflessly of her friendship, which brings with it never ending love and support. Also for her strong belief in me when I was lost, broken and had no belief in myself, at all!

And last, but certainly not least, I thank my dear friend and mentor – Holly Nunan – for the effect she has had on my life since coming into it, and for having the key that helped me to unlock the limitless potential I hold within me. Thank you for encouraging and empowering me to fearlessly step up, and step out into my true power and purpose, and be seen!

Table of Contents

Introduction .... *i*

How to Use This Book .... *iii*

Part I *1*

Mindset Magick Exercise *1*

Part II *5*

Mindset Magick Morning Affirmations *5*

About the Author

Frances Douglas, also known as Franie D, lives on the beautiful Tweed Coast of the Northern Rivers of NSW, Australia.

Franie D has a strong ancient Irish background and magick has always been a part of her life and for the past 25 years she has formally studied energy healing, metaphysics and conscious healing and living.

She is an ordained Pagan Reverend, Usui Reiki Master, Genome Stem Cell Healing Master, Conscious Healing & Lifestyle Coach and Enrolled Nurse.

Franie D's mission in life is to help heal and balance the energies of the planet and its beings. She teaches about the importance of understanding what consciousness and energy are, and how to harness energy to manifest healing for the greater good of all.

Ultimately, she assists others to see their unique divinity and stand in the power of that, to enable them to have the most healthy, happy and successful lives possible.

Franie D is available for consultations – in person/phone/Skype and teaching. For further details, please contact:

Mob: 0439 815 010
Postal: PO Box 270
Bogangar NSW 2488
Web: www.franied.com

Introduction

My intention for this book is that it helps you start to find the sacred place that lies deep within you, where you recognise your divinity and limitless power.

May it have you basking in the glow of pure unconditional self love and the comfort of true and unconditional self acceptance. May it be the spark that ignites and inspires you to reclaim ownership of your life, and to realise the greatness of "you" and what you came here to achieve!

For many, many years I have worked on my own inner and outer personal development and growth. It has been an amazing rollercoaster of a journey, filled with passion, pain, joy, love, hate, failure and success. Most importantly, it has been an experience of growth, knowledge and healing of the physical, emotional, mental and spirit bodies.

During these years I have seen and used many methods of unlocking the doors of the unconscious and subconscious minds, both for myself and for clients.

How to Use This Book

The exercises in this book are two of the easiest, quickest and most effective ways of uprooting unconscious and subconscious negative core beliefs, and replacing them with new, positive beliefs about our self-worth.

Understanding how our mind and cellular DNA memory work together to either enhance or sabotage our actions, health and lives, is an interesting, but highly complex science.

A simple analogy that I can give you, is that our brain or mind is akin to a computer hard drive.

Certain programs are given to us all throughout our lives, but from conception to 7 years of age, our early childhood impressions regarding how to deal with core life issues are formed, becoming firmly embedded in our unconscious and subconscious minds.

They become so natural and familiar, we are not even aware that we are running on them.

Others, we pick up as we journey through our formative years and the carnival of life and its multitude of experiences.

Some belief programs are positive and highly functional to optimal health, wealth and happiness. But sometimes a thought or "program" that is negative or untrue and not congruent with our greater purpose is programmed into our "computer". It then becomes a negative unconscious or subconscious belief, not necessarily a true one. This then leads us to behave in ways that appear to sabotage our own health, happiness and success.

For example, if someone is told often enough that they will never be successful, then that will become their core belief on an unconscious or subconscious level. They might then self-sabotage any future opportunities that could lead them to success and fulfilling their purpose.

When a person has taken on negative programming, success just does not compute, and they will never be successful.

This IS NOT a conscious action of self-sabotage!

These deeply seeded unconscious and subconscious beliefs are what create flow or lack of it, in our lives.

Patterns of self-sabotage will continue on throughout one's life. Success will appear to be ever elusive, until the negative program is uprooted, deleted and replaced with a new and positive one.

Part I

Mindset Magick Exercise

The following exercise is a powerful tool to help uncover and uproot your unconscious and subconscious core beliefs or blocks.

You will need a pen, pad and timer.

Allow yourself some quiet time to sit and be still without any interruptions for about 30 minutes. Breathe 10 deep, conscious breaths, all the way in and all the way out.

When breathing in, your stomach should rise first, followed by your chest. When exhaling, your stomach should go down before your chest. Practise good, deep and conscious breathing.

Take the pen and pad, dividing a page into two columns.

The first column will contain three positive affirmations, each repeated three times. The second column will be the mind chatter that responds to your affirmations.

Set a timer for 5 minutes and start to write the affirmations in sets of three, over and over. Write the corresponding response from your mind chatter in the next column. When the timer rings, put the pen down and examine the mind chatter response!

If you feel that you are experiencing blocks or challenges in a particular area of your life, you can be sure that you have a negative core belief that isn't serving your greater and highest purpose.

These negative beliefs are rooted deeply in your unconscious or subconscious mind. For example, I am not good enough; I am not deserving; I am not a good spiritual person if I am materially abundant; I am not clever enough, etc.

Beliefs we hold will either help or hinder us with any sort of success. This could be in any area of our life, e.g. relationships, career, financial, health, home, etc.

If we can bring those beliefs to the forefront of our conscious minds, then we can delete and replace them with positive ones.

Once our subconscious is aligned with positive thoughts and intentions, it is inevitable that success will follow!

This is one of the most important links to being successful using the Law of Attraction. Your subconscious and unconscious must believe what your conscious mind is telling it – even if it has not yet come to pass!

The mind chatter responses will show you exactly what your subconscious core beliefs are, by bringing them into the conscious mind.

Example:

Affirmation: I have a successful multi-million dollar business!

Mind Chatter: That's a lie!

Affirmation: I have a successful multi-million dollar business!

Mind Chatter: You aren't clever enough!

Affirmation: I have a successful multi-million dollar business!

Mind Chatter: You don't deserve that!

Affirmation: (Your name) has a successful multi-million dollar business!

Mind Chatter: No you don't!

Affirmation: (Your name) has a successful multi-million dollar business!

Mind Chatter: You couldn't achieve that!

Affirmation: (Your name) has a successful multi-million dollar business!

Mind Chatter: You are really poor!

Affirmation: (Your name), you have a successful multi-million dollar business!

Mind Chatter: No, I don't!

Affirmation: (Your name), you have a successful multi-million dollar business!

Mind Chatter: That's not possible!

Affirmation: (Your name), you have a successful multi-million dollar business!

Mind Chatter: I'm not clever enough to have that!

Repeat this exercise every day until the mind chatter affirms and confirms the Positive Affirmation.

Example:

1st Affirmation: I have a successful multi-million dollar business!

Mind Chatter: I can do anything when I believe in myself!

2nd Affirmation: (Your name) has a successful multi-million dollar business!

Mind Chatter: Yes! I am a very successful woman/man!

3rd Affirmation: (Your name), you have a successful multi-million dollar business!

Mind Chatter: Yes! I most certainly do!

Repeat this as many times as is needed, until the mind chatter confirms your affirmations.

Once you have done this, you can then start to cement this new program into the subconscious. As you fall to sleep every night, say the three affirmations, three times each, as a meditative mantra.

As you have uprooted the negative core beliefs that weren't serving you in your life journey, you don't have to be as consciously mindful of the mind chatter as when you were doing the Mindset Magick Exercise.

You know that whatever the mind chatter is saying is confirming and affirming your new positive conscious beliefs and thoughts.

The affirmation can be related to any area of our lives we are experiencing challenges or blocks.

The 1st Affirmation is always in the first tense.

Example: (I) have ...

The 2nd Affirmation is always in the second tense.

Example: (Name) has ...

The 3rd Affirmation is always in the third tense.

Example: (Name), you have ...

Part II

Mindset Magick Morning Affirmations

For thousands of years, Consciousness Masters have achieved elevated states of Conscious Awareness, through a daily practice of deep conscious breathing, meditation and visual focus.

Focusing on something that is visually pleasing, while simultaneously focusing on deep breathing, can calm the spirit and provide a sense of soul peace.

This section of the book is designed to give you a beautiful visual and powerful positive affirmation to focus on for 31 days.

I have compiled a collection of my favourite photographs of sunrise, from my own personal photo collection.

This is a time of day for re-birth, and we can easily feel wonder, peace and be inspired.

Each daily photograph is accompanied with a powerful affirmation. However you are free to use any affirmation you feel is best for you and your desired outcome.

Personally tailoring your own affirmation is very powerful!

Day 1

I release ALL resistance to standing in my true and authentic power, now.

Day 2

I believe in my self and my self-worth flourishes, with each new day!

Day 3

With childlike faith, I know I am safe and surrounded by love and support, always!

Day 4

I create my own reality with love and claim back my infinite power, now!

Day 5

I now allow the Universe to bring to me its abundance – on every level, and I receive it with gratitude!

Day 6

I welcome this day with the innocence, faith, joy and wonder of a child!

Day 7

Perfect health is my Divine right
and I claim it now!

Day 8

I am light ...
I give light ...
Everything around me shines!

Day 9

I trust that everything is happening in perfect Divine timing, for the greater good of all, whether I understand that in this moment, or not.

Day 10

My whole being is in perfect health and harmony.

Day 11

I embrace every experience in my life and know it is perfect for my greater good and growth!

Day 12

I choose to forgive everyone from my past who has hurt me. I thank them for the growth the experiences brought me! I release all pain connected, now!

Day 13

As I move beyond forgiveness and into understanding, I have unconditional love, compassion and kindness, for all!

Day 14

Each new day comes with a fresh, new opportunity. This new day is the first day of my new life!

Day 15

When I enter a room my presence lifts people's spirit, like a gentle summer breeze!

Day 16

I am a harmonious being. I have perfect balance in my mind, body and soul!

Day 17

I am perfectly imperfect and it is my imperfections that make me a uniquely beautiful soul!

Day 18

Today I will let go of a past that does not serve me and create a future that does!

Day 19

In order to see all the opportunities and new beginnings around me, I now choose to let go of ALL bitterness, anger and resentment!

Day 20

I am a magnet that attracts an infinite abundance of money and I am open to receive it, now!

Day 21

I am willing to change and grow for my greater good and the greater good of all, with ease and grace and harm to none!

Day 22

As I look in the mirror I am willing to see my magnificence!

Day 23

I am open and receptive to a fabulous relationship that meets ALL of my needs and wants!

Day 24

My life is full of abundance in every way!
I am now fulfilled and free to do whatever
I wish to do, with ease and grace
and harm to none!

Day 25

I believe that the rest of my life will be the best of my life!

Day 26

Every single one of my cells is now well and filled with health and vitality and innately knows what to do to heal!

Day 27

I am grateful for my healing and am now healthy, happy and whole!

Day 28

I am open to wonderful new challenges, because life only brings me great experiences!

Day 29

I love and accept myself
unconditionally, right now!

Day 30

I am worth the time I spend on my healing and joyfully nourish my mind, body and soul!

Day 31

Abundance is my divine birth right!

Magick (noun):

Ceremonial ritual or witchcraft, spelled with a "k" to differentiate it from sleight of the hand or illusionist magic. (Spelling attributed to Aleister Crowly)

'The art of changing consciousness at will.'
– Dion Fortune

True magick is neither illusion nor make believe, but an extension of imagination, emotion and will, used for the art of transformation – whether it be material or spiritual!

I have known Frances Douglas for 13 years. In that time I have had some great life challenges to face and deal with. I am so thankful and grateful to have had her to go to for counsel and guidance, in my darkest hours, during those years.

Before she came into my life, I felt lost, hopeless, helpless, alone and very depressed. I wanted to feel happy, successful and in control of my life, but I didn't know how to get there.

After Franie came into my life, shared with me her wisdom and taught me ways of dealing with life's curve balls, my life and happiness took an upward swing.

I felt happier and healthier. My relationships with others improved! My life meant something to me again and I was able to "let go" of negative emotions from painful past experiences and therefore, see and focus my energy towards all of the positive experiences that surrounded me.

It is difficult to find the words to express the love and gratitude that I feel for this awesome woman! Without her and her wisdom, love and continued support, I feel I would have remained "lost" in a very dark world!

Victor Mulvihill, Tree Arborer

I have known Frances Douglas for several years now and I have gone to see her for healing, on many occasions, during those years.

Her guidance, counsel and energy healing sessions helped me to overcome deep depression and anxiety.

When I first met her I had very low self-esteem. I felt scared, alone and very sad, anxious and depressed.

After my visits with Franie, I always felt so much better – lighter and happier! She helped me to regain my self worth and self-confidence and to overcome the depression that I felt.

Recently, she has shown me a new breathing technique to help me deal with panic attacks and anxiety that has really helped. It is so simple and I can do it anywhere and at any time.

I am so grateful to Franie for her patience, compassion and for the healing and wise guidance she has given me. I know that I am now the healed, happy and confident woman that I am, as a direct result of her being in my life and the help she has given to me.

Vivien Dorrough, Aged Care & Disability Nurse

www.ingramcontent.com/pod-product-compliance
Lightning Source LLC
Chambersburg PA
CBHW040003110526
44587CB00001BA/35